JAPJI:

MEDITATION IN SIKHISM

JAPJI:

MEDITATION IN SIKHISM

Translation and Commentary by
Swami Rama

The Himalayan International Institute
of Yoga Science and Philosophy of the U.S.A.
Honesdale, Pennsylvania

©1987, ©1996 by the Himalayan International Institute
of Yoga Science and Philosophy of the USA
RR 1, Box 400, Honesdale, PA 18431-9706

Third Printing 1998

The paper used in this publication meets the minimum requirements of
American National Standard for Information Sciences—Permanence
of Paper for Printed Library Materials. ANSI Z39.48-1984. ⊚

ISBN 0-89389-107-X

Contents

Foreword

Guru Nanak, the founder of Sikhism, belonged to the Bhakti movement of the fifteenth century along with such fellow travellers as Kabir, Ravidas, Jaidev, Namdev, Farid, and several other saints. They strove to heal the strife-torn socio-political fabric in India, menaced with Hindu ritualism and Muslim fanatacism. Guru Nanak launched his mission with a modest call, asking the Hindus to be good Hindus and the Muslims to be true Muslims. However, the compulsions of the times galvanized his followers into one of the most scientific faiths among the religions of the world today.

An unparalleled crusader of his time, Guru Nanak was an inborn verse writer. He employed his talent as a poet to carry his message throughout the length and breadth of the subcontinent, nay even to Sri Lanka and Lakshdweep in the south, Manasarover in the north, the Holy Mecca and farther to Baghdad in the west, and the borders of Burma in the east. He has bequeathed a substantial volume of divine verse which has been preserved in the *Holy Granth*, the Sikh Bible. Of all his scriptures *Japji* is considered to be his most outstanding work, containing the quintessence of the Sikh philosophy and prescribing the Sikh way of life.

Written in Punjabi, the language of the common man of the land of Guru Nanak's birth, *Japji* has been rendered into English in part and whole by such eminent scholars as M. A. Macauliffe, Dr. Gopal Singh, Khushwant Singh, Professor Gurbachan Singh ("Talib") and a number of others. However, I believe that no matter how well done, no work is translated for good. It applies even to the *Holy Bible*. Every generation has to make its own translation of the classics and other works of importance. The idiom changes, the images acquire different shades, the words shed their old connotations. Not infrequently a people read themselves in a translation. They like themselves to be reflected in their rendering of the original. It is said, "Every text is original because every translation is different."

It is a truism that many of the best poems in the Western languages are in translation, and yet it is maintained that poetry does not lend itself to being rendered into another language. Robert Frost described poetry as "what gets lost in translation." The poet may not have been wrong, but there are exceptions to the rule. Edward FitzGerald demonstrated it in his handling of Omar Khayyam's *Rubaiyat*. Swami Rama does it once again with his rendering into English of *Japji* by Guru Nanak.

It is because, rather than attempting mechanical rendering, both FitzGerald and Swami Rama capture the spirit of the original text. Swami Rama has the added advantage of belonging to Guru Nanak's order. A man of God, he has drunk deep at the fount of the spiritual heritage of India, living the greater part of his life with the Himalayan masters.

Swami Rama was commissioned by Gudhri Baba, one of his preceptors, to render into English the Sikh scriptures so that the holy word would be propagated far and wide. A blessed soul, the devotee in the author has made an excellent start. His rendering of the *Sukhamani Saheb*, the Psalm of Peace, another masterpiece from the Sikh scriptures, is to follow before long.

The Sikhs are in ferment today. They are a greatly misunderstood people. Translation is a vital integrating factor. It helps demolish citadels of cultural isolationism. It fosters understanding and brings people closer. It enriches a language and widens the sympathies of its readers. It brings the knowledge and experience of the whole world to one's doors. This is exactly what Swami Rama's enchanting translation of Guru Nanak's *Japji* is going to do both for the Sikhs domiciled abroad and the non-Sikhs of the English-speaking community.

Swami Rama's skillful handling of the English idiom is matched only by his deep devotion to the Sikh Guru's teachings. A kindred soul, he seems to have entered into the spirit of Guru Nanak's holy verse. We have, therefore, in this volume a version of *Japji* that surpasses all earlier attempts at rendering this great poem into English.

The text of the translation is preceded by a thought-provoking dissertation on meditation as conceptualized by the Sikh scriptures. Who could do it better than Swami Rama, a renowned spiritualist of international repute, a Vedantist of deep learning, and a devotee of Guru Nanak?

Swami Rama's earlier work, *Celestial Song/Gobind Geet*, presenting the dynamic dialogue between Guru Gobind Singh, the tenth Sikh Guru, and Banda Singh Bahadur, has already carved for him a niche in the galaxy of the celebrated students of Sikh studies. His rendering of *Japji* and *Sukhamani Saheb* should hopefully lead the poet in Swami Rama to continue the holy task of rendering the Sikh scriptures into English and thus earn the gratitude of the Sikh community for ever and ever.

K. S. Duggal

Preface

It was in 1947, after I returned from Tibet, that I was directed to travel and visit some of the rare saints of the Sri Nanak Dev order. I visited all the holy places and conversed with many great souls in the Himalayas. I traveled with a sage, a great *jnani* who was famous for his way of life. He was called Gudhri Baba. I have never met anyone else who would recite the *Adi Granth* verbatim in one posture. He had memorized the entire *Adi Granth*. Such rare great men are not known by historians, writers, priests, and intellectuals. It was Sri Gudhri Baba who said that I would have to one day write on *Japji* in a practical manner. The way he explained *Japji*, the sacred book of meditation in Sikhism, in that same way I submit this commentary for the use of meditators.

I am not a great poet but I like to rhyme and the rhyming in this book was done in a simple way. It was done so that children would be able to remember *Japji*, and adult aspirants would practice in a methodical manner. Actually, *Sri Sukhamani Saheb*, the Psalm of Peace, authored by Guru Arjan Dev, the fifth Sikh Guru, should have preceded it. It is already at the press and I feel sad that it was not released earlier. Soon it will be available. The price of this book has not been set to make a profit, but has been arranged in such a way that it is available at cost as a service to aspirants.

I have tried not to distort the original text in translation, while rendering it in a simple meter called loose iambic tetrameter. If there are any mistakes in this text I apologize for them. I hope that aspirants will find this book useful, for the research on meditational methods contained here is based on my own experiences and experiments.

Acknowledgments

I express my feeling of gratitude to Mahimah, who helped me to prepare the basic text on *Japji*. I equally appreciate and admire the effort of Kevin Hoffman and Rolf Sovik in checking the meter and giving vital suggestions. I thank Kamal for final typesetting, Vicki Roser for layout, and Gopala Deva for printing. Dr. Clarke also has gone through this book carefully.

Sing the Name of the Lord

Sing the name of the Lord in every breath of life.
Joy, joy, joy. . . . . Let me offer you
The finest of intoxicants, a drink that can subdue
All pain and inner suffering, no matter how obscure.
This drink I recommend to you, its value I assure.

You drink the cup of worldly wine, and sing a song
   you know,
Your drink creates a drowsiness, your song but
   augurs woe.
I offer you a wine divine, a melody so pure,
Your soul will wake, immersed in joy, and with
   my thought concur,

That God's name strikes an inner chord of harmony
   and bliss.
The infinite, the timeless, God created you for this.
The melody of japa sung with breath and in the
   mind,
No truer song than this can any concert artist find.

So take the name, and sing the song, and let your
    heart be cleansed.
Make the moments deep that you with your
    divine Self spend.
The japa might be heard as prayer, a kind of inner
    pleading,
But no, let it resound within, fill your entire
    Being.

Aum is the form, and one Holy Name true, of the
    sound of love Divine
Of the awesome, amazing, Supreme Guru,
    the source of Thee and Thine.
So repeat these words in your heart to imbue,
    the Vision of God everlasting:
Ek Omkar Satanam Sri Wahe Guru

Sing the name of the Lord in every breath of life.
Joy, joy, joy. . . .

Invocation to Japji

Mul Mantra

Ek Omkar	The One Reality
Sat Nam	Eternal Name
Karta Purukh	Creator Principle
Nirbhau	Without Fear
Nirvair	Without Abrasiveness
Akal Murat	Eternal Form
Ajuni	Unborn
Saibhang	Self-Existent
Gurprasad	Known by Guru's Grace

Japa	Remember His Name
Adi Sach	True in the Beginning
Jugadi Sach	Has Ever Been
Hai Bhi Sach	Is True Now
Nanak Hosi Bhi Sach	Nanak says:
	Ever Shall Be Eternal

As it was in the beginning: the Truth;
So always has it ever been: the Truth;
Likewise in the present is it: the Truth;
And throughout eternity shall it remain: the Truth.

Sri Guru Nanak Dev
The first Sikh guru (1469-1539)

PART 1

Japji:

Meditation in Sikhism

Throughout the lengthy span of Indian civilization, saints and sages have declared the divine nature of the human spirit, and have fathomed the Reality within. The Sikh gurus are representatives of this universal tradition. Through their meditation practice they came to realize the Truth and to manifest it in their time. The methods of meditation practiced by the great sages form a complete science of self-transformation and self-discovery. Through meditation one learns to explore the deepest levels of one's being and to know the center from which consciousness flows. The systematic practice of meditation has never been limited to a particular era in history or to any individual culture. It is given by the wisest of humanity for all times, cultures, and races. Meditation is an essential method for attaining peace and harmony both within and without.

What Is Meditation?

The word "meditation" is frequently misunderstood. While all the great spiritual traditions of the world have arisen from meditative experience, over time the practice of meditation has been neglected. "Meditation" has become a word without a clear definition or meaning.

We might understand meditation better through the use of a simile. When the turbulence of waves and undercurrents makes it difficult to peer beneath the surface of a body of water, then what lies below remains unknown. At

3

such times even if lovely coral were to sparkle at the bottom, or the water's bed were strewn with jewels, these treasures would be obscured. One's vision would be blocked by the ripples and the cloudiness of the water.

The individual human mind is like a body of water. Consciousness, the Atman, is a jewel shining within. To know the jewel of consciousness is to reach the highest goal of life—yet the mind remains tossed and turned. For most people there is no systematic method for understanding one's own mind or for calming its disturbances. As a consequence the limitless beauty of human life remains unsought, and therefore undiscovered.

Meditation is not primarily a method of contemplation or of prayer. There is a fine and subtle line of demarcation between meditation, contemplation, and prayer. In meditation awareness is focused inwardly. This focusing of attention follows a systematic path from the most external parts of one's personality, the body and senses, to the innermost, the mind itself. By treading the path regularly, the way becomes familiar and the mind is calmed and purified. Then the inner light of the Self begins to shine spontaneously—and life becomes a poem and a song.

Meditation is an experiential method. One who practices meditation becomes neither a slave to authority nor a pawn in the events of the external world. Instead, meditation allows the individual to think and act from his own most creative resource, the center of his own being. Through stillness, diaphragmatic breathing, the releasing of muscle tensions, breath awareness, and, finally, the resting of the mind in an internal focus, the meditator gathers experience of his own essence. Thinking, speaking, and acting from this inner perspective gives life a dynamic new meaning. The word "meditation," then, is actually somewhat like the word "medical," meaning "to attend." To meditate, one has to learn to attend to something with full devotion and commitment. By cultivating attention, by training the mind, one can begin to systematically understand the whole process of the inward journey. One has only to learn to be still physically, to have a serene breath and a calm mind.

The Body

The student should first learn to work with his body. The body is an essential instrument, but if it is not disciplined it can create barriers to progress. It is not that the body is something great that can transform one entirely. It is simply that if the body is not kept healthy, the mind is constantly distracted.

The first requirement of meditation is to be physically still, steady, and comfortable. Great strength comes from stillness and inner tranquility. If one learns to be still, he can enjoy a peace that cannot be provided by any object of the world. We are trained to prize the pleasures of eating, sex, and sleep, but no one imagines that stillness can give subtler joy. The art of stillness is not taught to us, but it can be cultivated.

To feel restful and still, it is very important to establish a steady and comfortable posture. These words, "steady" and "comfortable," are actually the words of the great sage Patanjali, who has used them to describe the correct meditation posture (*Yoga Sutras* II:46). The word "steadiness" means to sit so that the head, neck, and trunk

5

are vertically aligned and balanced. There are a number of postures that can be used for this. The simplest is to sit comfortably on the edge of a bench or flat-seated chair.

Many people misconceive the purpose of the meditation postures. They suppose that good posture has something to do with being able to twist the legs and put the hands and arms into certain positions. While a number of the postures with folded legs are comfortable for meditation, the intent of all the meditative postures is to arrange the body so that the spinal column is erect and comfortably aligned.

In the beginning, as one sits still he will observe that the large muscles of the limbs may jerk—something which often occurs to people as they fall asleep at night. Next, the muscles twitch—a second obstacle. When muscles twitch or when any part of the body throbs, these are not the experiences that manuals of meditation describe as signs of progress. These are merely a release of tension. The third obstacle that might arise is shaking. The body shakes or perspires because one is straining. If one tries too hard, or does not prepare his mind and accept the idea of meditation wholeheartedly, then he experiences mental strain. That mental strain can cause agitation in the body. So first the student should learn to assume the correct posture and not look for or think about having unusual experiences. After a few days he will observe that these throbbings, twitching, shiverings, and shakings have been arrested.

Breathing

Breath plays an important role in life. Both the body and the mind are disturbed by unregulated breathing—and both body and mind affect the breathing process as well. For example, bad news can start a person crying and sobbing. This results in great change in one's breathing patterns. Exercises like moderate jogging or brisk walking, on the other hand, can become means for deepening the breath. Learning to exhale twice the duration of inhalation—for example, while jogging, or between rallies in tennis—is a very healthy practice.

Stillness provides rest for the muscles and for the voluntary and involuntary nervous systems. Relaxed diaphragmatic breathing further strengthens the involuntary nervous system and establishes a balance between the intake and the output of the lungs. It is not healthy to retain waste gases in the lungs; doing so allows substances to build up in the body which may cause disease. A balanced flow of breath, with inhalation and exhalation approximately equal, is an essential prerequisite for progress in the meditation process.

The natural breathing pattern, called "diaphragmatic breathing," is everyone's birthright. Diaphragmatic breathing in itself gives very significant benefits, and it is a necessity if one wishes to practice any other breathing exercises. The diaphragm is a muscle lying beneath the lungs. During inhalation it contracts, creating the effect of expanding the areas at the base of the rib cage and just below. During exhalation, when the abdomen is gently contracted, the diaphragm relaxes and breath flows out.

Shallow breathing occurs because of shallow thinking, shallow habits such as eating too much, and a lack of activity, as well as a pattern of not being accurate, exact, or direct in life. Because of their habits, people lose the natural capacity to breathe diaphragmatically, and this results in self-created suffering. But it is easy to practice diaphragmatic breathing. To perform it, one should lie down on his back, feet and arms slightly apart, in the corpse posture, and put a small sandbag on the abdomen. Normally twelve to fifteen pounds is the recommended weight necessary to strengthen the diaphragm for adults. Once the habit is formed, it is no longer necessary to use the sandbag. Keeping the head, neck, and trunk aligned and the lips closed, one should exhale, allowing the abdomen to contract. Let the upper abdomen and base of the rib cage expand naturally with the inhalation. Do not create muscle blocks. If this is practiced three times a day, one will be a totally transformed person in a month's time, thinking differently and feeling very energetic.

These experiments have been repeatedly and successfully conducted in the Dana Research Laboratory of our Institute. Dr. John Clarke, a well-known cardiologist from the Harvard School of Medicine, and Dr. Rudolph Ballentine, a psychiatrist and famous nutritionist, experimented on many subjects. They discovered that diaphragmatic breathing, though a preliminary step, is most essential before practicing the higher rungs of breath awarenesss.

A second useful study was undertaken by Dr. John Harvey, Pandit Dr. Rajmani Tigunait, Dr. Phil Nuernberger, Dr. Kay Gendron, Duncan Currey, and Doug Bill. They formed a group to investigate the effects of breathing exercises. They found that diaphragmatic breathing was beneficial for calming the mind before meditation. They also noted that diaphragmatic breathing could be employed in daily life, and that this breathing was very useful for maintaining emotional balance.

Proper breathing means that the breath is not shallow,

jerky, or noisy, and that there are no lengthy pauses between the exhalation and inhalation. Noisy breathing is a symptom of blockage or obstruction. Long pauses in the breath mean that one is high-strung and has emotional problems. Such pauses are not created when people are happy, but occur when they are experiencing some agony, problem, or insecurity. There is a brief natural moment between inhalation and exhalation, but it should not be expanded by bad breathing habits. Such a pause, if unnecessarily expanded, can be a killer; it can create coronary heart disease.

Application of Sushumna:
How to Make Breath Harmonious

The mind itself does not want to meditate because it has not been trained to maintain a relaxed focus. Gradually one can understand and train the mind. If one learns to be still and to breathe well, then next one can attain a state of mind that is called "the joyous mind." In the technical language of yoga, this is called the application of *sushumna*. It is the method of leading the mind to a state of joy, where true meditation is possible. Sushumna application means that the breath is made to flow equally through both the nostrils. When one understands the basic breathing exercises, then he should pay attention to the breath flowing through the nostrils. When he becomes sensitive to the flow of the breath, he will usually find that one of the nostrils is obstructed. The right channel of breath is called *pingala* and the left is called *ida*. These are the heating and cooling systems in the body; the right and left channels act to balance heat and cold respectively.

Sometimes one of the nostrils remains open excessively,

while the other remains obstructed. This dominance of the flow of breath in one nostril reflects an imbalance. Those whose left nostrils flow excessively are depressed and emotional, accustomed to thinking about death and negative things, feeling insecure, and crying frequently without any reason. Those whose right nostrils flow excessively tend to think constantly of doing active things, such as drinking or fantasizing about sex. The sages say that by focusing the mind on the bridge between the two nostrils, one can bring the breath under conscious control, creating balance. Unless one brings these two vehicles of inhalation and exhalation under conscious control, the mind will be disturbed by unregulated breathing.

For meditation, neither the left nor right channels should be dominant. If one inhales and exhales equally from both, he cannot think of anything negative. The mind will find this experience delightful—an inexplicable state of joy. Such joy has no external cause; it does not come from the love of any object. In this state of temporary joy, called sushumna application, one can easily lead the mind into meditation.

Fluctuations in one's meditation from day to day are often associated with irregularities in nostril dominance. This relationship can be deceptive, because nostril dominance is in turn affected by one's habits. Excesses in regard to food, sex, or sleep, and the play of fears in the mind, can all create imbalance in the breathing pattern. Fear in particular should be analyzed. Fear is an attempt to escape, but the objects which create fear have never been thoroughly examined. Fears invite danger. They arise from the instinctive urge for self-preservation. When fears are examined, then anxiety is reduced and often dissipated altogether. By examining all thought patterns carefully, useless habits and irregularities can cease to be a distraction to meditation.

Meditation

The essence of the meditative method is to learn to objectively observe whatever comes into the mind by being mindful. To do that, the mind needs an object of concentration and an inner point of focus. The mental object for concentration is called a mantra. It is a word, syllable, or sound—or a set of words, syllables, or sounds—that protects and guides the aspirant on the inner journey. A mantra is not chosen haphazardly. The spiritual teacher gives the aspirant a mantra appropriate for his particular personality and stage of development.

For those who do not have a teacher, the sound *so-ham* may be used. "So" (pronounced with a lengthened "o") means "that which I am in my own being," and "ham" (pronounced like the English word "hum") is a verb form meaning "I am." These two sounds respond to the flow of breath—"ham" on the exhalation and "so" on the inhalation. The sounds "so" and "ham," when observed in the mind along with the breath, lead to a calm inner focus. Exhale, and think in the mind "ham"; inhale, and think in the mind "so." By focusing on this mantra the mind is made strong, secure, and one-pointed.

Sat Nam Sri Wahe Guru, the shorter version of the *mul mantra* in Sikhism, is inhaled and exhaled constantly with the breath. This helps the aspirant in forming a habit and finally making that which is called *ajapa japa* (soundless and automatic remembering of the mantra) a part of daily life. Guru Nanak Dev highly recommends these practices of inner remembering.

Japji: Meditation in Sikhism

Guru Nanak Dev gives a beautiful saying:

Nanak dukhiya sab sansar
So Sukhiya jis nam adhar.

(Nanak says: In this world everyone is miserable. Only he who has his foundation in the Name of God has joy.)

This explains how important it is to remember the Lord of Life in every breath. Through this practice the city of life remains in a state of tranquility. A tranquil mind is the finest of tools we can have to be successful in the external world and peaceful within.

There is a special term used in the meditative training: *japa*. It is from this word that the title of Sri Nanak Dev's work has been taken. The literal meaning of japa is "to remember." Mere repetition of the mantra, without deep feeling, helps in the formation of habit patterns but does not lead the aspirant to the highest goal.

The human personality has a particular character composed of habit patterns. Habit formation plays the most prominent role in our behavior. The mul mantra is complete in itself, touching the gross, the subtle, and the subtlest aspects of one's being. When the mul mantra is remembered regularly and punctually, during the early morning and evening hours (considered the finest hours for meditation), then the next state, which can be termed "soundless sound," is attained.

There is a higher state than mentally remembering the mantra, a fully conscious state in which the entirety of mind is absorbed and a single feeling alone exists. This feeling leads the aspirant to the fountainhead of life and light, *Omkara,* which is the aim of the meditator. *Om* is the mother sound, perennially self-existent in the cosmos and within human life. It contains its own form, which is why it is called *Omkara.* All the sounds have their own forms, but the form of the *Omkara* is limitless, timeless, and infinite; therefore it cannot be conceived by the mind or the senses. But it can be attained in the deepest state of meditation.

The first step is to constantly remember the mantra. The second step is to remember the mantra with a singular feeling of love and devotion. In the third stage, japa becomes an unconscious habit. One is busy doing his duties and japa is simultaneously going on. This is not a dual state of mind, but one in which japa takes over the human mind and one simply goes on doing his duties. This is called meditation in action, *ajapa japa.*

In the fourth stage, feeling deepens, which swallows all other interrupting thoughts and feelings, and the sound is absorbed by the great blissful silence within. This can be termed *anahata nada,* the unstruck sound, the voice of silence. In such a state the aspirant attains a state of oneness with the cosmic sound, *Omkara.*

Every word of the mul mantra, starting with *Ek Omkar Sat Nam* to Gurprasad, has profound meaning, so these words should be pronounced mentally with reverence. When the entire human being becomes an ear, then he hears *Omkara.* One can never imagine such a joy unless he directly experiences this stage.

Ek means "one." Here it refers to that infinite and eternal Reality that is One and Absolute without a second. That One is self-existent and ever deathless.

Omkara is the mother sound, perennially hummed in

the cosmos. *Sat Nam* is used because among all the names and forms of the animate and inanimate, the word *sat* is the highest. *Sat* means "essence"; *sat* alone is self-existent, not subject to change, decomposition, or decay. *Nam* means "name." The Truth is infinite and eternal, and to attain this Truth the grace of the guru, who is accomplished and one with the Divine, is required.

Sri signifies the feminine gender, singular in number. It represents the feminine principle of the universe, the first cause of the manifestation of the universe, without which the universe cannot exist.

The phrase *Wahe Guru* is also profound. The word *wahe* means "awesome." *Guru* is a combination of the words *gu* and *ru; Gu* means the darkness of ignorance, *ru* means the light of knowledge: that knowledge which dispels the darkness of ignorance is *guru.*

There are four aspects of grace. The grace of the *Adi Granth* is received by reverently repeating the sayings. The grace of God is equally important. The third, the grace of the guru, leads a student to a state of freedom from the bondage of karma and *sanskaras.* The fourth aspect is the grace of the self. If the aspirant does not have his own grace, he cannot retain the grace of the guru, of God, or of the *Adi Granth.* Therefore, before expecting to have the grace of God, guru, or the *Adi Granth,* one should tap the resources within oneself. *Sankalpa*—a full zeal for attainment, a burning desire, a perennial fervor, and a burning flame—should be lit.

A still and steady posture, a serene breath, regularity in practice, an even mind, and firm faith are the preliminary steps. If a room has been dark for millions of years, it can nevertheless be lighted in a second's time by the grace of the guru. It is true that when the disciple is ready, the knowledge of the guru dawns.

To do japa in the fullest sense of the word, one should remember the mantra over and over again with full devotion and a one-pointed mind. The space between the two breasts, the sacred heart or *anahata chakra,* is considered to be the focal point which in time leads the aspirant to a state of tranquility and equanimity. For attaining that state of equanimity one needs to do preliminary work punctually, with daily regularity, and with full faith and devotion.

The aspirant may also be given a personal point of focus. If one is physically sick, then the navel center or solar plexus *(manipura chakra)* is the focal point for meditation. If one is very emotional, then he can concentrate on the heart center *(anahata chakra),* the space between the breasts. If one is intellectual, and always inclined to reason or analyze, then the space between the eyebrows *(ajna chakra)* is the proper focus. If one is creatively inclined, the hollow of the throat *(vishuddha chakra)* is the point of concentration. These focal points for meditation should not be chosen for oneself, however; they should be given by one's spiritual guide. Then one can focus the mind on the proper chakra or point, rather than identifying with his thought patterns.

Learning to witness the thinking process is an essential skill. When one learns to witness something, then he can really enjoy and understand it. But when one becomes emotionally involved, identifying himself with his thoughts, he forgets his true self.

One can learn to fathom all the levels within. This is very helpful and healthy, because eventually a time of transition comes when no one else can be of help. At death, one cannot completely communicate his inner experiences to anyone—not to doctors, therapists, friends, spouse, children, or other dear ones. At that time, the tongue does not move; the eyes want to see, but there is a haze over all, and fearful darkness creeps upon one and takes over. One must be realistic and prepare for that day. If one learns how to remain uninvolved with the objects of the world, then the transition from life to death will become easy.

Meditation means physical stillness, serene breath, and freedom from identification with the objects of the mind. Through meditation one learns to understand the self and the not-self, and to enjoy the here and now. However, meditating for five minutes a day and then being irritable the whole rest of the day is not going to help anyone. Meditation in silence should lead to meditation in action during the day. Because spiritual teachers instruct their students to meditate for five or ten minutes a day, the students expect themselves to be transformed into perfect beings. But that is not possible without meditation in action. No matter how many teachers say that students can transform themselves with meditation in stillness alone, they are misleading their students.

Five or ten minutes of meditation is very healthful provided one also commits himself to being aware of meditation in action throughout the day. One should remember the goal of remaining uninvolved and disidentified with the objects of the world, with his feelings of attraction and aversion, and with the other thought patterns in his mind. If one gets involved in these things, he becomes biased and prejudiced, and his effectiveness is lost. Therefore one should learn to practice meditation within and without.

The Jewel Within

Words and images are part of the flow of the conscious mind. Modern culture invests its resources in training this conscious mind, and the colleges and universities of the world are almost exclusively devoted to such training. When one examines such a training process it is easy to see that modern education is incomplete. It leaves individuals with all their physical and emotional tensions uncared for. Humanity has forgotten how to resolve its pain, and seems habituated to feelings of self-doubt, uncertainty, and petty egoism.

The philosophy of meditation offers a very beautiful alternative, based on practical experience. When one begins to train oneself in the meditative process, he finds that conflict, pain, and sorrow have no eternal validity. This world is like a constantly changing show of colors. When the mind grasps a color, it becomes stained. Through meditation, clarity and vibrancy of the mind are recovered and one learns to know that the true inner nature of a human being is eternal, unchanging, and free of pains and miseries.

Knowledge of this pure being, which actually lies beneath and within the conscious mind, is true wisdom. In the beginning it takes a little courage to begin the voyage from the known to the unknown. It is easy to remain stuck in the patterns of one's own thinking process. The wise aspirant does not try to make sudden leaps, but takes the advice of the meditation teacher to train his habits at all levels—body, senses, breath, and mind. Then meditation gradually leads the aspirant beyond external joys and pains to that eternal joy. The great ones of the world have ever maintained this serene vision, experiencing the innermost jewel that shines in the inner chamber of one's being.

A Universal Method

It is clear that the method of meditation is not any ritual belonging to any particular religion, culture, or group. The unbroken tradition of meditation, stretching back over fifty centuries, does not oppose any religion or culture. Westerners are sometimes frightened by meditation and think that it proposes a new and conflicting view of religion. They have forgotten the message of the Bible, which says, "Be still, and know that I am God." Similarly Sikhs, Hindus, Buddhists, Jains, and believers of all parts of the world will find meditation to be a scientific, systematic, and necessary method for exploring inner truth.

For seeking truth in daily life the methods of contemplation must also be employed. Though the schools of meditation and contemplation are different, they both can help a student go beyond and establish himself in his own essential nature. When such basic ideals as truthfulness and non-harming are pondered and then applied in daily life, it is called "contemplation." These great ideals of humanity are shared equally by all religions. Further, we believe that all great religions have come from one and the same absolute Truth. While contemplation is a seeking and searching for truth, meditation is practicing and experiencing this truth. Meditation leads to wisdom and to the accomplishment of the purpose of life.

Benefits of Meditation

We all expect to be peaceful, we all expect to have

18

happiness within us, and that is why we like to enjoy things. Even the smallest enjoyment comes with the hope of finding peace within. Clearly, many suppose that happiness within can be obtained by finding happiness in the external world. Another alternative is to gain external happiness by cultivating a happy attitude within. Through meditation one can do both. One can be happy in the external world through one's attitude toward conducting one's duties and speaking and acting in that world, and at the same time one can maintain happiness within by constantly remaining aware of that Reality that is beyond the body, senses, and mind. Meditation allows one to understand the real source of happiness within and without.

All the scientific attainments in the external world, all the comforts of modern life, can benefit us if we view them as means and not as ends. Having a proper attitude is essential. Modern people suffer from many self-created diseases such as hypertension, ulcers, migraine headaches, and depression. The cause of these lies within the mind, and when the mind is trained through meditation practices, meditation becomes a useful therapy in daily life for the prevention of many psychosomatic diseases.

When the mind and its modifications are controlled through meditation, one can enjoy inner serenity and do one's duties efficiently. Through meditation alone can one consciously come in touch with one's hidden potentials. To become creative and dynamic, meditation is very important. A successful meditator is never unbalanced by the problems of life, nor tossed by the charms and attractions of the world. A meditator remains unaffected in all circumstances of life, good or bad. Through meditation, every human being can do tremendous good for humanity.

Scientific Experiments

It is useful to note the extent to which modern science has become interested in meditation. Many recent experiments have demonstrated the benefits of meditation practice. Studies have indicated, for instance, that meditation can be helpful in relieving fears and phobias, in reducing common forms of hypertension, and in helping people to relax.

Recent studies have begun to examine the unique changes occurring within an individual's consciousness during the meditation experience. These studies suggest that in addition to the physiological, emotional, and cognitive benefits of meditation, there is a subjective range of experience that laboratory instruments cannot capture. Subjects in meditation experiments report that they have experienced positive internal states which seem a rich and promising source of inner knowledge. Analysis of this phenomenological data is further making scientists aware of the need to study the vast and relatively unexplored literature of the meditative traditions.

Freedom from Stress

The challenges and problems inherent in modern life cannot be avoided by anyone. There will always be difficulties to face in the flow of life's events. What is missing in modern life is a balanced philosophy of action and inner wisdom. It is important for every human being to know that a reservoir of strength and beauty lies untapped within.

Meditation offers a hopeful answer to problems of

stress because it very carefully examines the human personality at all levels. The nourishment of the body, the regulation of deep and relaxed breathing, the establishment of positive mental dialogues with oneself, and the drawing of the mental focus toward one point of restfulness, all contribute to make meditation a complete approach to the problem of stress management. Meditation encourages individuals to become self-aware and self-responsible. It offers a wide variety of personal skills that help to free one from the pains of self-created misery.

Meditation Makes One Creative

The highest potential of human life can be attained through meditation. When an aspirant first begins to tread the path, however, he must learn to transform slothful and egotistical tendencies. In the early stages of practice it is important to observe one's habits and to gradually gain freedom from harmful attachments and aversions.

In the beginning it is also common to find that one does what was not intended and fails to do what was intended. The mind returns to old habits, despite one's sincere desire for change. This demonstrates that willpower is lacking, that our attraction to the highest and purest emotions and thoughts is not yet sufficiently strengthened.

Through internal resolve, the clinging nature of the mind is gradually weakened. One begins to enjoy meditation more and to yearn less for objects of sense experience. Soon the mind reflects in its choices in the outer world a growing tendency toward selflessness, contentment, giving and caring for others, and attraction for that which is spiritually elevating. Whereas ordinary people become

21

attached to their duties and the fruits received therefrom, aspirants are motivated to perform their duties with equanimity, for the benefit of others. Thus a stage of practice develops in which one becomes creative and is able to act with inner determination and sovereignty. Creativity is reflected in the mind's natural capacity to use the objects of the world as means and not as ends in themselves. The creative mind acts wisely for the benefit of the many, with freedom from the compulsions of attachment and aversion. Such a mind observes the interplay of the forces of nature that shape every action and reaction. By yielding when yielding is prudent, and acting decisively through the faculty of discrimination, the creative mind makes the world a vehicle for crossing from one shore of disappointment and delusion to the other shore of perennial bliss.

The Self of All

The individual self is called, in the meditational philosophy, the *jiva*. Each jiva, each individual self, maintains its characteristic separateness from the other selves of the universe by its association with a particular vehicle called the unconscious. The unconscious is like a reservoir, storing the impressions of past thoughts, spoken words, and actions. By the habitual association between consciousness and these latent mental tendencies, a personality is manifested to the universe and sensed from within as "I," the individual ego.

Through meditation, one comes to understand and to experience that the mind is a whole, containing many levels and functions, and that subtle aspects of the mind can be employed to guide the individual ego on its path of self-discovery. This inner guide, the *buddhi*, is awakened and strengthened through meditation. As long as the self uses the unconscious as a vehicle, it is called jiva, but the moment the self renounces the vehicle, it is called pure consciousness. The ancient scriptures say that the great sages in deep meditation and the highest state of tranquility came in touch with this superconscious state and thus experienced the profound knowledge and wisdom of the timeless, eternal, infinite Truth. This knowledge is higher than any other source of knowledge, and through such deep inner experience a person of wisdom realizes, in this very life, the Self of all.

Sri Nanak Dev, the First Sikh Guru

In his time, Guru Nanak Dev (1469-1539) reminded the people of the ancient message of human spirituality. His was an exemplary life. The son of Hindu parents who lived near Lahore, he remained occupied with spiritual matters from his youth onwards. Guru Nanak Dev was not lulled into the spiritual passivity of the surrounding culture. He valued devotion and skillful action, and translated his own deep realization into a life of service and social commitment.

Most of the sages of the meditative orders led their followers, disciples, and students on the path of renunciation. Guru Nanak Dev, being a householder, established that anyone leading a householder's life and conducting all his duties in the world could meditate and thus be useful for himself and others. This vivid theme marks the difference between Guru Nanak Dev's teachings and the teachings of other sages.

He gave hope and security to householders and common

people, recommending that meditation be practiced by all. He discouraged renunciation and said that householders are not inferior to any renunciate. Such teachings should be forcefully propagated and spread far and wide. Guru Nanak Dev established an ideal for his followers in which the health and endurance of the body, mind, and spirit are equally maintained. Among Sikhs moderation, purity, and selfless service were uplifted. Formalism, useless ritual, excessive mortifications, intolerance, and bigotry are all absent from the teachings of Guru Nanak Dev. He beautifully said:

> The throne of God exists in all places;
> His treasure house fills up all spaces.
> God, being Truth, lights up all faces.

In short, Guru Nanak Dev expounded the ideal of a fully civilized person who lives holistically, with inner awareness of the Lord and with the purpose of serving the nation selflessly. Hail to Guru Nanak Dev and his teachings.

Meditation in Sikhism

Without any commentary, the poetry on *Japji* of Guru Nanak Dev reveals its meditative origins. From beginning to end, the words of the *Japji* express a deep longing and devotion for realization. Just as the Sikh tradition finds its source in the songs and images of the divinely inspired guru Sri Nanak Dev, so these songs in turn find their origin in meditation, and proffer the way of meditation to any who might follow his path.

The following verse from a later portion of the *Adi Granth* reflects the deep source of this meditative message:

At the point of ecstasy
the song divine is sung.

The self is cleansed and listens
as the unstruck bell is rung,

All desire dissipates,
the mind with God's name thrilled;

Disturbance gone, in silence
is one's very being filled.

One's senses all complete their task,
the mind is safely bedded.

Nanak slaves for him in whom
the self with Self is wedded.

From this it is clear that meditation is the cornerstone of the Sikh religion.

The mantra *Sat Nam Sri Wahe Guru,* which forms the basis for the Sikh practice of meditation, is the shorter version of the mul mantra.

In the mul mantra, *Ek,* the numeral "1," expresses the fundamental unity underlying phenomenal reality. Before multiplicity, before manifestation, according to Sikh philosophy, is nondual Reality. The second word of the text is the meditative mantra *Omkar,* or *Om.* Here Guru Nanak Dev provides the means for knowing the underlying Reality: the recitation of the name of God, or *Om.* In this first pair of syllables Guru Nanak Dev lays the spiritual foundation for all that is to follow in his instruction to his disciples. He exhorts his students to know the Reality by remembering the name of the Divine in heart and mind.

This instruction is not the dry and sterile message of

intellectualism, nor is it a fanatical, self-righteous appeal. In meditation one rests one's mind in the nectar of inner concentration. It is nectar-like because by focusing upon this inner sound the mind finds comfort and can at last merge with the Infinite. Thus in the second pair of words, *Sat Nam,* the individual is exhorted by Guru Nanak Dev to understand that the name of God, *Om,* "alone is true and real."

The opening words of the *Japji* are traditionally completed by the phrase *Sri Wahe Guru.* These words are a symbol of obeisance. They pay homage to the trinity of forces in the universe, and to the Unmanifest from which these have evolved.

It is accepted that Guru Nanak Dev practiced the highest form of spirituality. He notes the difficulties in training the mind and conquering unruly passions, and also recommends the threefold stages of experience: that is, listening to the guru, pondering or contemplating upon what has been heard, and finally realizing Truth through meditation or japa. These, he suggests, are the right means for attainment. To these he adds the act of remembering the holy name of God (*japa*) and devotion. According to Guru Nanak Dev all interests, attitudes, and practice find their completion in divine service. Each aspirant lives in consonance with the duties and oportunities for service that unfold naturally in his own life.

In the last full stanza of the *Japji,* stanza 38,the meditative message of this text is confirmed. Here Guru Nanak Dev stresses the importance of daily meditation and by a metaphor conveys how the proper attitudes for meditation can be remembered and cultivated. He speaks of continence as a goldsmith's workshop, patience as the goldsmith, austerity as the heat of the goldsmith's fire, and the devotee's love for God as the crucible. Then he continues:

> Forge your enlightenment in this holy space;
> The Divine has sent meditation as grace.

According to Guru Nanak Dev, the grace of happiness dawns upon those who practice meditation daily.

In the near future a commentary on the *Sukhamani Saheb* will offer further insight into the Sikh meditative tradition. The Sikh path of devotion, service, and wisdom is a noble path. May the poetic and meditative words of the *Japji* inspire all those who walk along it.

PART 2

Japji:

The Poems of Japji

Invocation

The One Reality
Eternal Name
Creator Principle
Without Fear
Without Abrasiveness
Eternal Form
Unborn
Self-Existent
Known by Guru's Grace

Remember His Name
True in the Beginning
Has Even Been
Is True Now
Nanak says:
Ever Shall Be Eternal

As it was in the beginning: the Truth;
So always has it ever been: the Truth;
Likewise in the present is it: the Truth;
And throughout eternity shall it remain: the Truth.

1

The nature of God eludes the soul
Who seeks through thought the final goal.
In silent trance, though eons spent,
Mind's restlessness may not relent.
The desire of man may never cease
Though wealth and worldly goods increase.
From a thousand, nay million, feats of mind
No closer is man to God sublime.
How then for man to be pure in soul,
Transcend illusion, and achieve the goal?
Nanak says:
Self-realization requires surrender
To the pre-ordained will of God, the defender.

2

By divine command all forms manifest:
Unfathomable, unthinkable, is the Lord's behest.
Souls dwell in their bodies by His command;
Some lowly, some exalted, and others grand.
Divinely ordained, men are made high or low;
By his order they live in joy or sorrow.
Upon some, by His order, grace is bestowed,
While others must tread transmigration's long road.
All of the worlds by His law are controlled;
None can escape His sustaining hold.
Nanak says:
If man would only embrace God's command,
Egoless, noble, and free would he stand.

3

Men who've caught glimpses of God's infinite power
Sing of His might; o'er all men does He tower.
Those who have seen the signs of His grace
Sing of His blessings, of His exalted place.
Some sing of God's grandeur, of His noble deeds,
But His grace and greatness words' power exceeds.
Some men sing in praise of His wisdom and light,
But full vision eludes man; his mind is too slight.
Some say He forms bodies, then returns them to earth,
Say He takes life away, then allows for rebirth.
Some praise God's transcendence, His vision so clear;
Some sing of His presence, how He is so near.
Upon this earth there will ne'er be an end
To the millions of songs in God's praise men will send.
Eternally does He His creation sustain;
Endlessly giving, more than man can contain.
Nanak says:
According to His order the universe shall be;
Yet He is ever in bliss, untouched and carefree.

4

The Lord is holy; His name is true.
Countless devotees sing His virtue.
Men ask of God His gifts to provide:
Ever reliant, He has always complied.
What can we offer to God in return
And how a glimpse of His court may we earn?
What words shall we utter to God above
In order to win His favor and love?
Nanak says:
Utter His name at the hour of dawn;
Reflect on His greatness: His love will be drawn.
Man's actions determine his next incarnation;
God's grace leads him on to the door of salvation.
Nanak says:
Live by His order; worship His feet.
Know God is absolute, true, and complete.

5

Established by no one, created by none,
God alone is pure, the self-existent One.
Nanak says:
Honor is gained by serving the Lord;
Sing praise to Him, and His grace afford.
Sing praise and remember His name from the start,
Then nurture a love for Him deep in your heart.
All pains of His devotees He will dismiss
And finally give entrance to the mansion of bliss.
Under His guidance His own name is heard;
With wisdom acquired, His grace is conferred.
The word of the guru is a mystical sound—
In its wisdom and light does the whole world resound.
Guru, Shiva, Vishnu, and Brahma is He,
and Parvati, Lakshmi, and Sarasvati.
If, by grace, were I to fathom the Lord,
How could I describe Him, most blessed, adored?
By what means could His greatness e'er be expressed?
The subject for now cannot even be addressed.
My master has explained one truth to me:
There is but one Giver and it is He.
He the provider for all mankind;
Let His name ever linger, suffusing my mind.

6

Eagerly would I bathe at each holy place
If this would earn me the favor of His grace.
But if these ritual acts do please Him not,
Of what their use? Let them all be forgot.
Among created beings that I may behold,
Good deeds prompt good fortune to surely unfold.
Diamonds, rubies, and pearls, their light brightly glows
Upon hearing the words that the Guru bestows.
My master has explained one truth to me:
There is but one Giver and it is He.
He the provider for all mankind;
Let His name ever linger, suffusing my mind.

7

If the life of a man could span four ages full
And persist ten times longer past death's heavy pull,
And if his fame spread to all the earth's corners,
And masses bowed down and became his adorners,
If his life lacked the grace of God's touch,
Then even with men, his worth couldn't be much.
Worm among worms—his rank would be less,
An object of pity unless he confess.
Nanak says:
The Lord alone to man confers worth,
But none can grace Him who are of this earth.

8

Absorbing His teachings and hearing His name,
Mẻn will gain salvation and freedom from pain.
Opening mind and soul to His wisdom divine,
Men will know the mysteries of His kingdom sublime.
Then will come understanding of the nature of earth,
Its support, the high heavens, and man's own special berth.
Knowledge of all regions will be obtained
When one's mind with God's teaching is fully ingrained.
Listening to His name and absorbing His teaching,
Men shall pass from the grasp of even Death's reaching.
Nanak says:
With true joy in their hearts, the saints ever reside;
Sin and sorrow abandoned, in God's name they abide.

9

Learning divine teachings, man will become
As Shiva, Brahma, and Indra, absorbed in the One.
Listening to God's name, recalled in the heart,
Uplifts the lowly, and gains them a start.
The Lord's name absorbed in the heart will reveal
Secrets the mind and the body conceal.
And in the same manner insight is gained
Of scriptures, philosophies, and knowledge unnamed.
Nanak says:
With true joy in their hearts, the saints ever reside;
Sin and sorrow abandoned, in God's name they abide.

10

Truth, contentment, and wisdom are gained
When the sound of God's name has been deeply retained.
The merit of bathing in pilgrimage places
Is matched by absorbing His name and His graces.
Men attain honor who hear and who read
God's name and His teaching; for they will succeed.
By absorbing His name, the heart finds repose;
The mind becomes fixed, to realization exposed.
Nanak says:
With true joy in their hearts, the saints ever reside;
Sin and sorrow abandoned, in God's name they abide.

11

By absorbing His teaching one fathoms deep pools
Of spiritual virtue, imbibing God's rules.
Titles of Sheikh, Pir, or Saint should soon be obtained
By those in whose hearts God's pure name has remained.
So, too, men of blindness, envy, and wrath
Find spiritual sight when they follow God's path.
Those carrying God's name in their hearts fathom deep
In the ocean of bliss where God's secrets e'er sleep.
Nanak says:
With true joy in their hearts, the saints ever reside;
Sin and sorrow abandoned, in God's name they abide.

12

The state of pure faith is so indescribable,
The attempts to express it are far from reliable.
Despite dedication of man to his pen,
Faith looms above thought and the words of men.
Only when faith in God's name is most firm
Can one behold the Absolute and His truth confirm.

13

When through faith man is able to focus his mind
Then the knowledge of all realms and all spheres he
   will find.
Rooted in faith, he need never contend
With the merciless judgment of death at life's end.
Nor will he suffer fierce blows to his face;
Hereafter, he'll live in the arms of God's grace.
He who obedient to the word of God lives,
Gains in his heart what faith alone gives.
Only when faith in God's name is most firm
Can one behold the Absolute and His truth confirm.

14

Man's path to enlightenment shan't be obstructed
If with faith and devotion his life is conducted.
With honor from this world he'll surely depart,
Shining in faith, and happy in heart.
Firm in devotion, he'll walk the straight way
In search of truth; he never will stray.
Only when faith in God's name is most firm
Can one behold the Absolute and His truth confirm.

15

Living in faith, with full concentration,
Man will arrive at the door of salvation.
By his example a man of true love
Takes his kin with him to find God above.
The guru devoted, swimming 'cross life's wide ocean,
Carries with him disciples, in the wake of his motion.
Nanak says:
A man of true faith need not beg or plead;
God will surely provide for his every need.
Only when faith in God's name is most firm
Can one behold the Absolute and His truth confirm.

16

Approved by God are saintly men and for His court
   appointed.
They meditate on His True Self, their soul with light
   anointed.
In Light they have their joy, in describing God their
   pleasure—
But God's works are indeed beyond the ken of human
   measure.
Dharma holds the earth and with contentment keeps the
   order.
How much the Bull of Dharma's load? The elect alone
   discover.
Beyond the earth are other realms: What power supports
   these stages?
The colors, names, and forms of things—God's pen writes
   all the pages.
But who accounts for all the forms? No human, it is
   certain:
God's power and His beauty lie behind His mystic curtain.
Vast creation 'rose from sound, wherein the million rivers
   flowed:
One word sufficed to manifest the limitless abode.

In light of His infinite power and might,
My power to describe him is ever so slight.
To him I cannot even a sacrifice be;
I stand before God, yet remain unworthy.
God is formless, infinite, and ever secure.
What pleases Him is good and pure.

17

Countless are the prayers, chanted with emotion.
Countless the meditations, in silent devotion.
Countless the methods of worship by men;
Countless the austerities that they have chosen.
Countless the chanters of the Vedas, reciting—
Endless their wisdom and love, delighting.
Countless the yogis whose minds have been turned
When, despite worldly life, God's name was learned.
Countless His devotees, deep in contemplation,
Seeking the final goal, God-realization.
Countless bestow worthy charity on others.
Countless are heroes, 'gainst their own hostile brothers.
Countless the worshipers who in their vow
Give steadfast devotion to God here and now.
In light of His infinite power and might,
My power to describe Him is ever so slight.
To Him I cannot even a sacrifice be;
I stand before God, yet remain unworthy.
God is formless, infinite, and ever secure.
What pleases Him is good and pure.

18

Countless are the foolish whose eyes cannot see.
Countless are the thieves, full of dishonesty.
Countless are the oppressors, using brute force.
Countless the cut-throats, killing perforce.
Countless the sinners entrenched in their crimes,
Repeating their evils o'er scores of lifetimes.
Countless are the liars, impure minds they maintain.
Countless the filthy seeking unlawful gain.
Countless the slanderers carrying in their heads
The nagging of others, both said and unsaid.
Thus Nanak, including himself in these classes
Talks of the wicked and ignorant masses.
To Him I cannot even a sacrifice be;
I stand before God, yet remain unworthy.
God is formless, infinite, and ever secure.
What pleases Him is good and pure.

19

Countless are His spaces, countless are His names,
Countless and inscrutable His worlds and His aims.
To term His realms countless, a man incurs sin,
For trying to measure His greatness therein.
Through words the name of God is said;
Through words, His praises sung and read.
Through words the holy texts we learn
And so His wisdom we discern.
By letters written on His head
The destiny of man is said.
His holy union with God is foretold,
Its way expressed so all may behold.
But though the words of God rule men,
Unmanifest is God's diadem.
What men receive is by God's order;
He is the giver and recorder;
He is everywhere, existing,
Ev'n in mind, always persisting.
How can words ever hasten our way,
When of His might scant words we can say?
To Him I cannot even a sacrifice be;
I stand before God, yet remain unworthy.
God is formless, infinite, and ever secure.
What pleases Him is good and pure.

20

If soiled are the body, the hands, or the feet,
With water a man can make cleansing complete.
Clothes that are dirty with soap soon will be
Rinsed of impurities, fresh, and dirt-free.
When man's mind is polluted with evil and sin,
His devotion alone can cleanse from within.
By his title alone a man has no gain;
One's actions are measured in an endless chain.
As a man sows, that crop will he reap—
During this life now, or in death's long sleep.
Nanak says:
It is God alone making each determination
Of who must continue in new transmigration.

21

Pilgrimage, austerity, compassion, and charity:
These give some benefit to man and some clarity.
But true merit requires full absorption of teachings,
Deep faith and devotion—and not mere beseechings.
By these means men bathe in the light of the soul,
Ever cleansing until they arrive at the goal.
All virtues and majesty live in Thee, Lord;
Myself, I have none—save those you afford.
Without the accomplishment of worthy deeds,
In devotion one never completely succeeds.
Salutations to Brahma, the transcendent One,
Who, with Maya's thread, his creations have spun.
His manifestation is the sacred Word:
May it nurture my soul and always be heard!
May I live with it always, and by grace perform
Loving actions for all, and my habits transform.
Truth . . . Beauty . . . God is all this—
Ever wise, pure, and free, and always in bliss.
What time, in what era—what date and what day,
What season and month—saw creation's first day?
None of the pandits have yet found the time,
Although to this theme the Puranas incline.
Nor have the Kazis revealed creation's hour—
Even the Koran is bereft of that power.

The yogis know not the day, month, or season:
The Creator alone knows the true time and reason.
How shall I sing to the Lord His own praise?
How shall I know Him or follow His ways?
Nanak says:
Of God and His qualities many surmise,
Each one regarding his theory as wise.
But He is the doer, He supreme and great.
And all that He wills comes to pass—it is fate.
Nanak says:
The proud, claiming power resides within them,
Find no honor above for this false strategem.

22

Millions of heavens and worlds He created;
Man's failure to count them has always been fated.
In search of God's limits men simply grow weary,
And cease their attempts, resigned to the query.
The Vedas affirm God's infinity
In a word that says all—"neti, neti."
Eighteen thousand species have now been confirmed—
But such count is absurd, where God is concerned.
The Muslim scriptures on this point are astute:
They acknowledge just One; the pure, Absolute.
To assess God's infinity many men try—
But before they complete the task, always they die.
Nanak says:
God is omnipotent, free, and all-knowing;
Offering His love, He is grace overflowing.

23

God's praises men sing, with steadfast devotion,
Though regarding His might they've an incomplete notion.
God is unfathomable, deep as the sea,
Receiving the rivers that flow constantly.
These waters (like men) are unable to know
The vastness into which they'll finally flow.
Eminent kings whose great power and might—
Extend across oceans, across day and night;
Whose wealth and possessions are truly immense;
Whose lives are lived out in extreme opulence—
Their worth is far less than the worth of an ant
Who in place of his own will, God's will would supplant;
Whose mind with God's name is devotedly filled;
Whose life with God's love is profoundly instilled.

24

Countless traits indeed mark God's singularity;
Countless His works, and boundless His charity.
He hears without limit; sees the unseen;
No one can know what His purposes mean.
Creation unlimited; endless domain—
The edge of His sphere men can't ascertain.
Men yearn to know His full power and capacity—
But His boundaries elude them despite their tenacity.
The more men attempt to discover God's bounds,
More deeply His infinite mystery confounds.
God is exalted, high-placed in His seat;
His name alone is what makes life complete.
Only a person as exalted as He
Could comprehend fully God's great mystery.
Nanak says:
Yet by His blessing and grace all men find
Love, and devotion, and true peace of mind.

25

How great is His bounty, men cannot record;
Provider, Protector, Benevolent Lord.
Great Giver is He who does selflessly serve
Without expectation, and with no reserve.
Infinite the men who put to God their request
For courage, and honor, and freedom from death.
Many spend lives in wicked endeavor.
Many take gifts showing gratitude never:
To receive a gift, and then this deny—
In so doing the highest of laws men defy.
Many suffer from poverty, age, and great pain:
These are His gifts, men should feel no disdain.
Freedom from the bondage of reincarnation
Comes only through grace and His determination.
About this subject nothing more may be said;
It is only by God's grace that we can be led.
The fool who seeks to interfere with God's plan
Will receive only punishment at God's command.
God alone knows what each man deserves
And by His sure knowledge His sentence He serves.
Few are the men who have offered Him gratitude;
Few have surrendered to His holy attitude.
Nanak says:
They to whom God grants the grace of devotion
Will be honored as kings and gain God's promotion.

26

Priceless indeed are His divine attributes;
Priceless the tradings that He executes.
Priceless the traders who, for His pleasure,
Acquire His goods and store His great treasure.
Priceless the buyers of His goods on display:
Priceless the devotees, carrying them away.
Priceless the praise and devotion that's rendered—
Priceless are men who to God have surrendered.
Priceless His justice, His court, His decrees;
Priceless His judgments, bringing men to their knees.
Priceless His blessings, His mark ever prime,
Priceless His grace, His ordinance sublime.
Priceless is He; His worth none can express—
But of those who do try there are some He may bless
With deep concentration to remember His name
And absorb them finally in His holy flame.
Vedic texts and Puranas—on Him do give focus,
While scholars give discourse and through
   speeches provoke us.
Brahmas and Indras speak of God the Divine;
To Him thoughts of Gopis and Krishnas incline.
Whether a Shiva, a yogi, or an enlightened soul,
All speak of His greatness and His splendor extol.

Demons and gods, renunciates and saints,
Attempt His description, not feeling restraints.
Many strive to express the great strength in His name—
But soon leave this world, without reaching their aim.
Should He then create twice the count into being,
Still He remains past describing or seeing.
Nanak says:
God is as great as He chooses to be,
And only He the full range of His power can see.
Anyone claiming to know the Divine
Thinks the ocean a puddle, and claims it as "mine."

27

Where is that portal and where is the mansion
In which God sits overseeing His expansion?
The notes of the music, the instruments too,
Like the players, are countless in praising His virtue.
Countless the symphonies, musical measures,
Countless the musicians, engaged for His pleasures.
Praising Him ever are fire, water, and air.
At His door, lauding Him, Dharmaraja is there.
The recorders of deeds for Dharmaraja to review,
Chitra and Gupta, His praises pursue.
Shiva, Brahma, and Devi shine by His grace;
In His mighty splendor, His song they embrace.
In the court of the gods, Indra sits on his throne,
Chanting praises to God, who is near, yet unknown.
Yogis and devotees, exalting in His song,
In meditation and in contemplation, to the Divinity
    belong.
Men of continence, truth, and contentment
Sing of His name with divine sentiment.
Unconquered heroes, men who are fearless,
Chant their fair songs to God, who is peerless.
Reading the Vedas, the scholars and sages
Repeatedly sing of Him throughout the ages.

Fairies beguile heaven, earth, and below,
Enchanting and charming with dance to and fro.
The Puranic jewels just reflect the Lord's graces,
As do the sixty-eight Hindu pilgrimage places.
All divine heroes, pillars of strength,
And the four sources of life, praise Him at length.
The continents, worlds, and the universe too,
Form a heavenly choir, a divine retinue.
They who can please Him, immersed in His love,
Sing of His glory both here and above.
Nanak Says:
Many more praise Him than I can e'er know;
Countless their number, a vast crescendo.
The Lord is above all, His name is true;
He is the creator of every virtue.
He the progenitor, now and forever;
Immortal is He, He will never cease, never.
He designed the world with all variations,
And now He beholds the vast range of creations.
Freely He acts, according to his pleasure.
None can command Him; His might exceeds measure.
Nanak says:
He is the King on whom all men rely:
All are subject to His will; this none can deny.

28

Let your earrings be contentment and honesty.
Let your begging bowl and purse stand for modesty.
Let ashes be symbols of your meditation.
Absorbed in God's name you'll achieve illumination.
Weave your coat tightly with thoughts of mortality,
Then don't lose sight of life's ephemerality.
Let the body be pure and throughout undefiled.
With your faith and God's name, make your life
    reconciled.
Make universal brotherhood your only sect.
Conquer the world through your mind's intellect.
Salutations to the One who is primal and pure,
Eternal, unchanging; who fore'er will endure.

29

Let your diet consist of Self-illumination,
Served with a love that commands admiration.
Let Divine music resound in your heart
So all life may listen and join in its part.
God is the true master; He plucks all the strings:
By His just command the whole universe sings.
All powers and wealth yield no satisfaction;
The desire for these will lead to distraction.
God alone governs man's union and separation—
According to destiny, man gets his just ration.
Salutations to the One who is primal and pure,
Eternal, unchanging; who fore'er will endure.

30

Maya in union with God gave birth
To three true disciples of unexcelled worth.
Brahma, Vishnu, and Shiva, the three:
Creator, Preserver, Dissolver they be.
By His Pleasure He governs the work that they do;
According to orders, they carry it through.
Invisible is He to the eyes of these three—
But His vision sees them effortlessly.
Salutations to the One who is primal and pure,
Eternal, unchanging; who fore'er will endure.

31

God has His seat in all worlds of creation.
His treasures are boundless, beyond estimation.
After shaping the universe, pure and complete,
God maintains His creation, the one greatest feat.
Nanak says:
Holy indeed is His just administration;
Anchored in truth, His entire creation.
Salutations to the One who is primal and pure,
Eternal, unchanging; who fore'er will endure.

32

If for each one tongue, ten thousand would be,
And if twenty times that sung in full harmony,
Repeating God's name countless times without end,
The stairs of devotion he'd surely ascend.
Climbing higher and higher till finally he's done—
With the Lord Almighty at last he is one.
Even worms feel inspired this story to hear,
To reach heaven's splendor, by this path most clear.
Nanak says:
By His grace alone can a man Truth attain;
He who boasts of the false, his words speak in vain.

33

To speak or be silent is not in man's power;
Not for asking, nor giving, can man choose the hour.
One cannot direct how he lives or may die,
Nor gain wealth or power, though hard he may try.
To cherish God's name, or to do meditation,
Does not solely require man's deep concentration:
Neither by practice nor effort will man ever be
From worldly desires finally set free.
God alone is Supreme, the one power source;
It is He who acts only; men have no recourse.
Nanak says:
Before God the Witness all men are the same;
None are more worthy of praise or of blame.

34

God created nights, lunar days, weeks, and seasons,
As well as the elements and nether regions.
In the vastness of these He established the earth
As a harbor of righteousness, peace, and rebirth.
There He placed all beings of numerous kinds,
All differently named, with varying minds.
And they are all judged on the fruits of their actions;
God's wisdom sees all—the good deeds, the infractions.
The elect of God in His court find their place;
They bear the mark of His approval and grace.
Only at His court is false known from the true.
Says Nanak: Thereafter will judgment ensue.

35

Having explained thus the realm of right-minded action,
Now hear of true knowledge to your satisfaction.
In this realm, where true knowledge and wisdom are
    found,
Air, fire, and water, in all forms abound.
Countless the Shivas, whirling in dance;
Countless the Krishnas, singing their chants.
Countless the Brahmas, creating each world;
Countless the forms and colors unfurled.
Countless the opportunities for righteous action,
Celestial peaks to which gods find attraction,
Countless the Dhruvas, the sermons each hears,
Countless the Indras, the suns, moons, and spheres,
Countless the siddhas, the Buddhas, the yogis;
Countless the gods in great splendor and ease.
Countless the demons, and boundless each ocean,
Countless the jewels—in the seas' endless motion,
Countless creations and new forms of speech.
Countless the kings, who help, serve, and teach.
Countless are those absorbed in God's name—
Who serve, by God's grace, His own divine flame.

36

In this sphere of attainment and light,
Divine knowledge shines eternally bright.
Mystical vision and songs elevate
Inhabitants there to a most wondrous state.
That sphere of devotion is beyond compare,
So exquisite its beauty, its structure so rare.
What happens in that region man cannot say;
Lower mind and the senses fall by the way.
Attempting to speak what is beyond expression,
One soon becomes speechless, and offers confession.
In that sphere most mysterious one shall find
Absorption, wisdom, and enlightenment of mind.

37

The region of grace is distinguished by might:
There dwell powerful beings, of God's delight.
They are heroes, imbued with God's pure-burning flame;
They bathe in His light, and they dwell in His name.
Countless the heroines residing there,
Among whom is Sita, a saint beyond compare.
Those united with God, Maya never can tempt;
From death they are ever and always exempt.
Saints from all worlds reside in that grace;
With bliss in their hearts, God's light they embrace.
In this sphere the Lord Himself resides;
And in His glance all creation abides.
All continents, worlds, and all universes,
Are found in that realm, from where God's light disperses.
A count of the parts one can hardly pretend,
For as they're unique, so as well have no end.
There are worlds upon worlds—and even more still—
And all are obedient to His Divine Will.
He o'ersees and directs from His majestic place,
And casts His benevolent aura of grace.
Nanak says:
As hard as it is to force steel to bend,
Harder speaking of this, and this realm comprehend.

38

Shape continence into a smithy.
Let patience the goldsmith be.
Use as an anvil the illumined mind;
Of spiritual light let your tools be designed.
Fear God alone. Do not tire:
Make austerity the heat of the fire.
As a crucible, use devotion and love;
Remembering His name, draw in grace from above.
Forge your enlightenment in this holy space;
The Divine has sent meditation as grace.
Nanak says:
Blessed and happy are they in the dance
Who are mercifully graced by God's radiant glance.

Air is the guru; the father is water;
The mother is earth—as all would have thought her.
Day and night are the nurses who cradle creation;
In their laps the world plays in chiidlike elation.
God as the Judge watches how men do action;
He weighs the effects to His own satisfaction.
Man's actions determine his nearness to God;
Some travel ahead, others backward have trod.
Those whose consciousness radiates love of God's name
Will exit life humbly, acquiring that fame.
Their faces shall radiate divine love and light—
O Nanak, all men share their peace and delight!

Glossary

Adi Granth.   The sacred scripture of Sikhism. The compilation of the teachings of Guru Nanak Dev and many other sages of the tradition. After the guru lineage stopped with Guru Gobind Singh, the tenth guru, this scripture itself substituted for a living guru. It is the same as the Sri Guru Granth Sahib.

Ajapa japa.   An effortless repetition of mantra. After having practiced meditation regularly for some time, a student is able to maintain the awareness of his or her mantra all the time.

Ajna chakra.   The center between the two eyebrows, the seat of the mind. This center is called the "command" center, since at this chakra meditators receive guidance from above.

Anahata nada.   The voice of silence, heard by yogis in deep meditation.

Anahata chakra.   The heart center, from which yogis hear the voice of silence.

Atman.   The soul; the pure consciousness.

Brahma.   The Creator.

Buddhas.   Those who have attained the highest knowledge, Nirvana.

Buddhi.   The intellect, characterized by the powers of discrimination.

Chitragupta.   According to ancient texts, Chitragupta keeps records of all good or bad actions that human beings perform.

Contemplation.   Pondering upon and applying ideals such as truthfulness or non-violence in one's daily life.

Dharma.   The rules and laws which uphold righteousness and thereby help the human race to grow.

Dharmaraja.   The King of Dharma or righteousness.

Dhruvas.   A king and spiritual seeker mentioned in the *Srimad-Bhagavatam.*

Earrings.   Earrings, begging bowl, ashes, and coat refer to the lifestyle and belief system of a particular religious group, Kanphata yogis, who used to roam in northwestern India. Guru Nanak is advising them to internalize these external symbols and realize the truth within.

Ek Omkar Sat Nam Sri Wahe Guru.   There is only one Reality; OM is the eternal name; Hail to Sri Guru (who is identical to the Supreme Reality).

Four ages. In the Indian calendar, the whole cycle of creation is divided into four parts: Satya yuga, Trita yuga, Dvapar yuga, and Kali yuga. The present age falls in the Kali yuga.

Gods. Bright beings, celestial beings, those endowed with knowledge.

Gopis. Eternal consorts of Krishna.

Grace. The descending force of the Divine.

Guru. The spiritual master endowed with the capacity of dispelling the darkness of ignorance and leading seekers on the path of light.

Hatha yoga. A branch of yoga that mainly focuses on body and breath and serves as a stepping-stone toward the practice of raja yoga and kundalini yoga.

Hindu pilgrimage places. These are sites where great saints and sages lived for long periods of time, and are thus considered to be holy. Many of these sites are equally respected and visited by Sikhs and Hindus.

Ida. The left energy channel, which according to yoga manuals corresponds to the energy of the moon.

Indra. According to Indian mythology, the king of all gods.

Japa.   Recitation of a mantra and contemplation on its meaning.

Japji.   The Sikh book of prayers written by Sri Guru Nanak Dev.

Jiva.   The individual self.

Jnani.   A learned sage or a scholar.

Kazis.   Religious leaders of Islam.

Koran.   Holy scripture of Islam.

Krishna.   Mythologically, Krishna is an incarnation of Vishnu; it was Krishna who imparted the knowledge of the *Bhagavad Gita* to Arjuna.

Lakshmi.   The goddess of nourishment and prosperity; the consort of Vishnu.

Manipura chakra.   The center of shining gems, the navel center; also known as the solar plexus.

Mantra.   A sacred word with a profound meaning usually repeated and contemplated upon by meditators.

Maya.   Creative force of the Lord.

Meditation.   The unbroken focus and awareness on truth for a long period of time, without an obstruction.

Muslim scriptures. The Koran.

Mul mantra. The original mantra according to Sikhism. *Ek Omkar Sat Nam Sri Wahe Guru* is the mul mantra, the common mantra which every Sikh must practice.

Neti neti. "Not this, not this"; this phrase refers to the fact that the objects of the world are not real, rather God alone is real.

Om. The eternal sound which represents and is identical to the Absolute Reality.

Omkara. The same as Om.

Pandit. A learned scholar; one who knows the ancient texts.

Parvati. The daughter of the Himalayas, the eternal consort of Shiva.

Patanjali. A great saint and yogi who codified and systematized yogic practices and philosophies.

Pingala. The right energy channel, which according to yoga manuals corresponds to the energy of the sun.

Pir. A Sufi saint.

Puranas. Epic literature written in the Sanskrit language.

Puranic jewels. According to the epic texts, fourteen gems which appeared after churning the ocean.

Sankalpa. The power of determination and firm resolve in which one decides that he or she can and must do some action.

Sat Nam. The essence, the self-existent Absolute Reality which can be realized through the grace of the name of the Lord.

Sarasvati. The goddess of learning, the consort of (or sometimes referred to as the daughter of) Brahma.

Shastras. A group of scriptures that describe rules and laws on religious, moral, and ethical matters.

Sheikh. A Muslim saint.

Shiva. According to Indian mythology, the lord of annihilation.

Siddha. An accomplished master who, through practice and grace, has acquired higher powers.

Sikh religion. A religion expounded by Guru Nanak Dev and based on the authority of the Adi Granth or the Granth Saheb.

Sita.   Wife of Rama.

Smritis.   A group of scriptures that provide an essence of the Vedic teaching. Some of the Smritis are Manu Smriti, Namada Smriti, Lomasha Smriti.

So-ham.   A mantra meaning "I am That."

Sri.   Dynamic force of the Absolute Reality.

Sri Sukhamani Saheb.   A book of prayers most often recited in the morning.

Sri Wahe Guru.   "Homage to the great guru." This phrase most often occurs in the opening words of Japji.

Sushumna.   The central nadi through which the dormant force of kundalini arises and unites with supreme consciousness, Shiva, in *sahasrara*, the crown center.

Transmigration.   The cycle of birth and death.

Vedas.   The ancient scriptures wich embody the revealed knowledge of the sages.

Vishnu.   The Lord of protection.

Vishuddha chakra.   Center of purity and of space, the throat center.

Wahe.   The great, the most respected one.

Yoga Sutras.   The first systematic work of yoga science and philosophy, by Patanjali.

Yogis.   The aspirants of yoga; meditators.

About the Author

Yogi, scientist, philosopher, humanitarian, and mystic poet, Swami Rama is the founder and spiritual head of the Himalayan International Institute of Yoga Science and Philosophy, with its headquarters in Honesdale, Pennsylvania, and therapy and educational centers throughout the world. He was born in a Himalayan valley of Uttar Pradesh, India, in 1925 and was initiated and anointed in early childhood by a great sage of the Himalayas. He studied with many adepts, and then traveled to Tibet to study with his grandmaster. From 1949 to 1952 he held the prestige and dignity of Shankaracharya (spiritual leader) in Karvirpitham in the South of India. He then returned to the Himalayas to intensify his meditative practices in the cave monasteries and to establish an ashram in Rishikesh.

Later he continued his investigation of Western psychology and philosophy at several European universities, and he taught in Japan before coming to the United States in 1969. The following year he served as a consultant to the Voluntary Controls Project of the Research Department of the Menninger Foundation. There he demonstrated, under laboratory conditions, precise control over his autonomic nervous system and brain. The findings of that research increased the scientific community's understanding of the human ability to control autonomic functioning and to attain previously unrecognized levels of consciousness.

Shortly thereafter, Swami Rama founded the Himalayan Institute as a means to synthesize the ancient teachings of the East with the modern approaches of the West. He has played a major role in bringing the insights of yoga psychology and philosophy to the attention of the physicians and psychologists of the West. He continues to teach students around the world while intensifying his writing and meditative practices. He is the author of many books and currently spends most of his time in the mountains of Northern India and in Pennsylvania, U.S.A.

Main building of the international headquarters, Honesdale, Pa., USA

The Himalayan Institute

FOUNDED IN 1971 BY SWAMI RAMA, the Himalayan Institute has been dedicated to helping people grow physically, mentally, and spiritually by combining the best knowledge of both the East and the West. Institute programs emphasize holistic health, yoga, and meditation, but the Institute is much more than its programs.

Our international headquarters is located on a beautiful 400-acre campus in the rolling hills of the Pocono Mountains of northeastern Pennsylvania. The atmosphere here is one to foster growth, increased inner awareness, and calm. Our grounds provide a wonderfully peaceful and healthy setting for our seminars and extended programs. Students from around the world join us here to attend programs in such diverse areas as hatha yoga, meditation, stress reduction, Ayurveda, nutrition,

Eastern philosophy, psychology, and other subjects. Whether the programs are for weekend meditation retreats, week-long seminars on spirituality, months-long residential programs, or holistic health services, the attempt here is to provide an environment of gentle inner progress. We invite you to join with us in the ongoing process of personal growth and development.

The Institute is a nonprofit organization. Your membership in the Institute helps to support its programs. Please call or write for information on becoming a member.

Institute Programs, Services, and Facilities

All Institute programs share an emphasis on conscious holistic living and personal self-development. You may enjoy any of a number of diverse programs, including:

Special weekend or extended seminars to learn skills and techniques for increasing your ability to be healthy and enjoy life

Meditation retreats and advanced meditation and philosophical instruction

Vegetarian cooking and nutritional training

Hatha yoga and exercise workshops

Residential programs for self-development

The Institute's Center for Health and Healing, which offers holistic health services and Ayurvedic Rejuvenation Programs.

The Institute publishes a *Quarterly Guide to Programs and Other Offerings,* which is free within the USA. To request a copy, or for further information, call 800-822-4547 or 717-253-5551, fax 717-253-9078, email bqinfo@himalayan-institute.org, or write the Himalayan Institute, RR 1 Box 400, Honesdale, PA 18431-9706 USA.

Visit our Web site at www.himalayaninstitute.org.

The main building of the hospital, outside Dehra Dun

The Himalayan Institute Charitable Hospital

A major aspect of the Institute's work around the world is its support of a comprehensive Medical City in the Garhwal region of the foothills of the Himalayas. A bold vision to bring medical services to millions of people (most of whom are poor) who have little or no healthcare in northern India began modestly in 1989 with an outpatient program in Uttar Pradesh.

Today that vision has grown to include a large state-of-the-art hospital located between Dehra Dun and Rishikesh; a Medical College and nursing school; a combined therapy program that joins the best of modern medicine with the time-tested wisdom of traditional methods of healthcare; a rural development program that has adopted more than 150 villages; and housing facililties for staff, students, and patients' families.

The project was conceived, designed, and led by Swami Rama, who was a native of this part of India. He always envisioned joining the best knowledge of the East and West. And that is what is occurring at this medical facility, 125 miles north of New Delhi.

Guided by the Himalayan Institute Hospital Trust, the hospital, medical city, and rural development program are considered models of healthcare for the whole of India and for medically underserved people worldwide.

Construction, expansion, and the fund-rasing necessary to accomplish it all continues. The hospital is now one of the best-equipped in India, and attention is turning to building primary and secondary satellite health centers throughout the mountainous regions where travel is difficult, especially for those in need of immediate medical attention. Future plans include a college of dentistry, a college of pharmacy, and research facilities to study Ayurveda, homeopathy, and yoga therapies.

We welcome donations to help with this and other projects. If you would like further information, please call our international headquarters in Honesdale, PA at 800-822-4547 or 717-253-5551, email bmcinfo@himalayaninstitute.org, fax 717-253-9078, or write RR 1 Box 400, Honesdale, PA 18431-9706 USA.

The Himalayan Institute Press

The Himalayan Institute Press has long been regarded as "The Resource for Holistic Living." We publish dozens of titles, as well as audio and video tapes, that offer practical methods for harmonious living and inner balance. Our approach addresses the whole person—body, mind, and spirit—integrating the latest scientific knowledge with ancient healing and self-development techniques.

As such, we offer a wide array of titles on physical and psychological health and well-being, spiritual growth through meditation and other yogic practices, and the means to stay inspired through reading sacred scriptures and ancient philosophical teachings.

Our sidelines include the Japa Kit for meditation practice, the original Neti™ Pot, the ideal tool for sinus and allergy sufferers, and the Breath Pillow,™ a unique tool for learning health-supportive breathing—the diaphragmatic breath.

Subscriptions are available to a bimonthly magazine, *Yoga International,* which offers thought-provoking articles on all aspects of meditation and yoga, including yoga's sister science, Ayurveda.

For a free catalog call 800-822-4547 or 717-253-5551, email hibooks@himalayaninstitute.org, fax 717-251-7812, or write the Himalayan Institute Press, RR 1 Box 405, Honesdale, PA 18431-9709, USA.

Visit our Web site at www.himalayaninstitute.org.